The Way of Sa

A Slow Pilgrimage
from Dover to Canterbury

Guidebook

Liz Garnett

I would like to give a huge thank you to Alexandra le Rossignol for joining me on this and my earlier pilgrimage. Also, I would like to thank Marion Lynn, Sonia McNally, Mary Sampson, Annie Ross, Victoria Field, Vicky Morley and Kerry Donati for joining us on this adventure.

First published in September 2022 by Beechthorpe Press

Copyright © Liz Garnett

www.lizgarnett.com

Artwork credits: Liz Garnett

Wherever possible, I have tried to ensure historical facts are correct.

ISBN 978-1-7399484-2-9

Contents

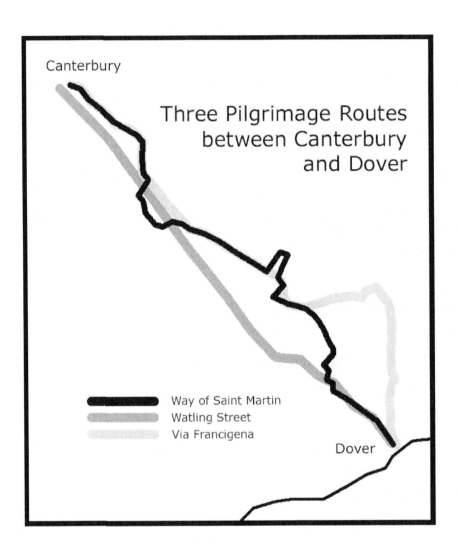

Canterbury

Three Pilgrimage Routes
between Canterbury
and Dover

Way of Saint Martin
Watling Street
Via Francigena

Dover

Introduction

After the success of their first pilgrimage following the Augustine Camino from Rochester to Ramsgate, Liz Garnett and Alexandra le Rossignol were invited by Martin Crowther of the Maison Dieu in Dover to create a new exhibition reflecting on the route pilgrims would have travelled from Dover to Canterbury. Both artists were keen to focus on the concept of a slow pilgrimage and a chance to get to know the area better.

Liz set about drawing up the route following the North Downs Way which encompasses the Via Francigena. It wasn't long before Liz and Alex were looking at adapting the existing route to include Barfrestone and Bishopsbourne. The route that Liz has designed also takes in the River Dour footpath in Dover and parts of the Elham Valley Way.

As research progressed into the development of this new pilgrimage route, Liz and Alex soon realised that the theme was becoming creative: Henry Moore was inspired by the church at Barfrestone and also lived at Kingston; the authors, Jocelyn Brooke and Joseph Conrad both lived in Bishopsbourne.

In medieval times pilgrims would not necessarily have followed a set route but would have taken any number of paths or tracks that would lead them to their destination. The most obvious one between Dover and Canterbury was Watling Street which now, mostly, lies beneath the A2 dual carriageway. Pilgrims would also have travelled in a variety of ways from foot to horseback to cart or carriage.

The area would also have been a busy trade route.

How to use this guide

Use this guide in combination with paper Ordnance Survey Explorer maps (Dover 138 and Canterbury 150) and/or the OS app. Ideally both. Maps and app are available from www.ordnancesurvey.co.uk. The app is particularly useful as it shows your exact location. The paper map acts as a back up should your mobile phone battery fail.

Throughout the guide there are opportunities to look out for interesting features or the natural world. Space has been left to add your own interesting finds.

Supporting the Local Community

Do support the local communities on this pilgrimage. From buying a drink in a local pub or cafe to putting a few coins in the donations box at a church, it all helps to keep the local communities alive. Churches that are open also have leaflets, postcards and guides to their buildings.

Slow Pilgrimage

A slow pilgrimage is about engaging with the environment. It is a chance to take the time to observe the landscape, town or village as you pass through. Take in the architectural detail on buildings. It is about seeing. Listen to the birdsong and watch wildlife, look up and look down, smell the blossom on the trees or smell the air after the rain.

The journey should be short as the purpose is not to cover vast distances but to appreciate what you see.

Liz Garnett and Alexandra le Rossignol developed this concept of pilgrimage for those who are not able to walk long distances. For them, travelling with fellow artists, the journey is about seeing through other's eyes. Each artist brings with them their own knowledge of nature, art and architecture and through observing and sharing. Each one of them has completed the pilgrimage with a greater understanding of the route than they would have done if they had travelled on their own.

The route from Dover to Canterbury is rich in history and they felt they were walking in the footsteps of medieval pilgrims travelling from the continent to Canterbury Cathedral.

Interior of Saint Edmund's chapel

Cross carved in church at Temple Ewell

Three Stories linked to the Route

The Trendyll Candle

In medieval times the citizens of Dover made a votive offering to the shrine of Saint Thomas Becket. The trendyll candle was a taper candle that was the length of the walls of Dover town. It was transported to the shrine at Canterbury Cathedral every three years on 6 July (the translation date of Thomas Becket). The candle was wound around a great reel and rolled from Dover to Canterbury via Bridge hill which is on Watling Street.

It is not certain why the candle was given as a votive offering. It may have been in response to the towns need for a saviour or as an act of thanksgiving. In Northern France and the Low Countries this type of offering was quite common in the late middle ages.

Choughs

Choughs are black crows with red feet and beaks which were once common in Kent but died out over 200 years ago. The Kent Wildlife Trust have teamed up with the Wildwood Trust to reintroduce them to the chalk grasslands around Dover.

Legend tells of how a chough dipped it's beak and feet in the blood of Thomas Becket as he lay dying in Canterbury Cathedral, turning them red. Three choughs were subsequently added to Thomas Becket's coat of arms. In the 14th Century, they joined the lion on the Canterbury City coat of arms. They also appear on the coat of arms of Saint Edmund of Abingdon.

They are mentioned in connection with Dover in Shakespeare's King Lear.

Hag Stones

Pilgrims arriving on the beach at Dover from the continent would collect a hag stone (a stone with a hole in it) and take it to Saint Edmund's chapel as an offering.

The stones are said to find you and you should only ever take one at a time. They are believed to have magical properties and ward off witches.

Countryside Code

Follow the Countryside Code to enjoy parks, waterways, coast and countryside.

Respect Everyone
- Be considerate to those living in, working in and enjoying the countryside.
- Leave gates and property as you find them.
- Do not block access to gateways or driveways when parking.
- Be nice, say hello, share the space.
- Follow local signs and keep to marked paths unless wide access is available.

Protect the Environment
- Take your litter home – leave no trace of your visit.
- Do not light fires and only have barbecues where signs say you can.
- Always keep dogs under control and in sight.
- Dog poo – bag and bin it – any public waste bin will do.
- Care for nature – do not cause damage or disturbance.

Enjoy the Outdoors
- Check your route and local conditions.
- Plan your adventure – know what to expect and what you can do.
- Enjoy your visit, have fun, make a memory.

Further information on the Countryside Code can be found at www.gov.uk/countryside-code

Decorative arch over doorway at Patrixbourne church

Face carving on north doorway at Barfrestone church

Things to Look Out For

	**Ordnance Survey Benchmarks** These are survey marks made my Ordnance Survey to record the height above the Ordnance Datum Newlyn. This is the national height above sea level for mainland Great Britain.
	Mass dials These are simple sun dials – a stick is placed in the hole to cast a shadow. The grooves in the dial indicated the times of masses.
	Choughs These birds are represented on many coat of arms in Kent. They are currently being reintroduced after an absence of 200 years.
	Butterflies The North Downs are an ideal place to view rare species of butterfly.
	Medieval graffiti Many churches have ancient graffiti and crusader crosses carved into their stonework.
	Hag stones These are stones with naturally occurring holes – normally flint. They can be found on the Downs and the beach at Dover.

Converted Mill in Buckland

Ruins of paper mill on the River Dour at Kearsney

The Area

Dover to Canterbury

Pilgrims have travelled from Canterbury through Dover and onto the continent on pilgrimages for centuries. The route from Dover to Canterbury became popular after the death of Thomas Becket with pilgrims travelling from the continent to visit his shrine.

Dover

Dover has been a key port in England because of it's proximity to the continent. Set in a valley fed by the River Dour, it has a rich history from the Bronze Age to modern times. The river has fed it's people and supported industries.

Dover's earliest known inhabitants were in the late stone age. They farmed the land. There are over 45 Bronze Age sites locally.

From about 762AD Dover's industrial heritage begins around the River Dour. This has continued throughout the centuries to include mills for corn and paper as well as breweries, tanneries and ironworks.

During the Roman era the town was thriving with a large harbour and two lighthouses on either side of the town. At the time the town was known as Dubris. The Romans developed Watling Street through Dover up the valley through Buckland, Kearsney and Temple Ewell. Watling Street had originally been built by the Celts.

From the 5th Century, the town was known as Dofras and was a major settlement in the new Kingdom of Kent.

After the Norman Conquest, Dover was rebuilt including the addition of new religious buildings Saint Mary the Virgin, The Maison Dieu and Dover Priory which now gives it's name to the railway station. The only remnants of the Priory are at Dover College and Saint Edmund's Chapel. During that time the port had a thriving cross channel traffic.

Dover played a key role during both world wars as well as being a target for bombings. In WWII, the majority of soldiers evacuated from Dunkirk passed through Dover and the town became famous for the song "There'll be Bluebirds over the White Cliffs of Dover" sung by Vera Lynn.

Canterbury

There has been habitation of the Canterbury area since palaeolithic times. The Cathedral, Saint Augustine's Abbey and Saint Martin's Church now form a world heritage site.

The first record of habitation is with a Celtic tribe who named the settlement Cantiaci. At that time the tribe inhabited most of what is now Kent.

The Romans captured the area in 43AD and rebuilt Canterbury in the 1st Century.

By the late 6th Century Canterbury was the capital of the kingdom of Kent and was ruled over by Ethelbert. It was at this time that Christianity was reintroduced to Kent by Saint Augustine.

The Bayeux Tapestry is believed to have been commissioned by Bishop Odo, the half brother of William the Conqueror. The tapestry depicts the Norman Conquest and it is believed to have been embroidered in England by women and created especially for the Bayeux Cathedral.

The North Downs

The North Downs are designated an Area of Outstanding Natural Beauty and are also recognised by UNESCO as a Global Geopark.

The unique landscape of the Kent North Downs is a biodiverse rich habitat which includes chalk grasslands, ancient woodlands, chalk rivers and dry valleys. It has the same geology as the champagne region of France with a growing number of vineyards being developed along the Downs.

It is one of the best areas in the UK for orchids with 25 out of 52 species being found on the Downs. Look out for bee orchids, pyramidal orchids and the common spotted orchid.

Villages and Hamlets

Kent farmland in this area mostly operated under a gravelkind tenure which is largely associated with Celtic law and continued in Kent after the Norman Conquest in 1066.

Coal Mining in Kent

Coal was first discovered in Kent in 1890 after the government halted the work on the first channel tunnel at Shakespeare Cliff. It was not until 1912 that coal with commercial value was raised to the surface. Nine collieries lived long enough to sink shafts and only four produced coal. One of the major problems was the undulating coal seams and the huge amount of water that flooded the mines. Snowdown colliery closed in 1987 and Bettshanger was the last Kent mine in 1989.

Historical Figures Linked to the Route

Saint Martin of Tours (c316 - 397)

Saint Martin was born in Hungary and is the patron saint of France, soldiers and winemakers. At the age of 10 he went to a Christian Church to help with mass and learn about Christianity. Even though he enlisted as a soldier in the Roman army at the age of 15, he remained a devout Christian. He is known for his kindness and, in particular, for offering his cloak to a beggar outside Amiens in northern France.

Saint Martin was baptized at the age of 18 and left the army to become a monk under the instruction of Saint Hilary at Ligugé outside Poitiers. Once instructed he went to Hungary to convert his parents to Christianity. His father refused to embrace the faith but his mother and many others became Christians. Saint Martin returned to France and built a small monastery outside the town walls of Poitiers where he lived and practiced austere penance. After the death of the Bishop of Tours he became his successor and had a monastery built near the town.

There are 3,660 churches dedicated to him in France. He was so popular that the pilgrimage of Tours preceded that of Compostella. He has been venerated since the 4th Century.

King Ethelbert (c506 - 616)

Ethelbert ruled the Kingdom of Kent. He was pagan and married Bertha, a Frankish princess from Tours in France. He established the first laws of the country which are contained within the Textus Reffensis which is held at Rochester Cathedral.

Queen Bertha (c539 - 612)

Bertha was a Christian and agreed to marry Ethelbert on the condition that she could bring with her Chaplain, Bishop Luidhard, to Kent when she married. She was given a Roman building as a royal chapel. This building is now the western part of the chancel of Saint Martin's Church.

Saint Augustine (d. c 604)

Pope Gregory sent Augustine to Kent at the request of Queen Bertha to preach and convert the inhabitants to Christianity as, after the departure of the Romans, most of the country had reverted to paganism.

Saint Augustine established an episcopal see and founded the church of Saints Peter and Paul which later became Saint Augustine's Abbey in Canterbury.

Saint Alphege (953 - 1012)

Alphege was an archbishop and first martyr of Canterbury. He was renowned for his austere life and care of the poor. In 1005 he became Archbishop of Canterbury where he was murdered by the Danes.

Saint Thomas Becket (1120 - 1170)

Thomas Becket's parents were married in Rouen, France in 1110 and Becket was born in London in 1120. He studied in Paris, Bologna, Auxerre and travelled widely in Europe.

Evidence suggests that Thomas Becket was a very human figure. When he was Lord Chancellor, he enjoyed a position of wealth and power. However, that all changed when be became the Archbishop of Canterbury in 1162 when he appears to have experienced some form of conversion and changed his ways. He took his new role seriously and turned to praying, fasting and being generous to the poor. He started to challenge the King and defend the rights of men as well as protecting the church.

After Becket was murdered, local people managed to obtain pieces of his cloth soaked in his blood. It soon became known that when touched by this cloth people were cured of blindness, epilepsy and leprosy. Soon the cathedral monks were selling small bottles of Beckets blood. He was canonized in 1173. His shrine was the first in Canterbury to draw pilgrims from Europe.

Records were kept of the miracles of Saint Thomas including one about a woman from Brittany who taught a starling to invoke Saint Thomas. When a kite seized the bird, it repeated the phrase and the kite dropped dead, freeing the starling.

Christians honoured Thomas as a martyr. Rich and poor alike pilgrimaged to his shrine including Louis VII of France in 1179 and Emperor Charles V of Rome in 1520. He wasn't just a saint for the English but also for Europe.

Many churches are dedicated to him. In Salamanca, Portugal, Corenno Plinio on the edge of Lake Como in Italy as well as one across the English Channel at Gravelines. Relics of Saint Thomas are held in the cathedral at Esztergom in Hungary. There is a window dedicated to Saint Thomas at Chartres Cathedral and there are mosaics of him in the Cathedrale of Monreal, Sicily.

Choughs are linked with Thomas and legend tells of how the birds dipped their beaks and feet in his blood when he lay dying in the cathedral.

At Canterbury Cathedral visitors can see where Thomas Becket was murdered and the site of his original tomb which was kept in the crypt of the cathedral between 1170 and 1220. His relics are now housed at Saint Thomas Church on Burgate, Canterbury.

Saint Edmund of Abingdon (1175 – 1240)

Saint Edmund of Abingdon taught theology at Oxford University before becoming Canon of Salisbury and then Archbishop of Canterbury. He was happiest instructing and teaching people in prayer.

Edmund dedicated almost all of his income to the poor and the church with miracles and conversions occurring after his speeches. He was made Archbishop of Canterbury in 1233 and was central to the relationship between Rome and England. He was critical of the king (Henry III).

In 1240, he gave up his office to become a monk at Pontigny Abbey in France and died later that year. Miracles at his graveside were soon reported and he was canonised in 1247. He later had the chapel in Dover dedicated to him. It was the first to be dedicated to him and the only chapel in England dedicated to one saint from another – Richard of Chichester, a long-term friend of Edmund. His cult was very popular in France.

Bishop Odo of Bayeux (c1035 – 1097)

Odo, Bishop of Bayeux and Earl of Kent, was the half brother of William the Conquerer. He was a strong supporter of William at the Battle of Hastings for which he gained a great deal of land after the invasion.

He features prominently on the Bayeux Tapestry and it is for this reason that it is believed that he commissioned it's creation. In 1082 he was disgraced and had his land and the title of Earl of Kent removed. He spent the next five years in prison. He died while on the first crusade and on his deathbed he was granted a pardon by William I.

Knights Templars

The Knights Templars were founded in the 12th Century after the first Crusades (1095 – 99) and were led by Hugues de Payens. They pledged to protect the holy places in Palestine and the visiting pilgrims who travelled there from all over Europe.

The crusades were a series of religious wars in the medieval period directed by the church in Rome. The most well-known ones were to the Holy Land between 1095 and 1291. The aim was to overturn the Islamic rule in Jerusalem and surrounding lands.

In 1127 Bernard of Clairvaux, a Cistercian abbot, created a rule of conduct based on the rule of conduct of the Cistercian order. He did much to promote the Knights Templar throughout Christendom and this helped to swell the ranks of the Templars.

They acquired property as an order and would establish a preceptory which would house a small number of 'brethren' who would collect rents and revenues as well as supervise the farming. The preceptory might have it's own chapel which might be round in shape as a special homage to the Holy Sepulchre in Jerusalem.

After the end of the Crusades, they were falsely accused of heresy and black magic. The order was finally removed of all its possessions in 1312.

Saint Edmund's chapel

Crabble Corn Mill

Creatives Linked to the Area

Geoffrey Chaucer (c1342 - 1400)

Chaucer was an author, poet and civil servant to the British court. His most well-known works are The Canterbury Tales about pilgrims travelling to Canterbury.

William Shakespeare (c1564 - 1616)

Shakespeare was a playwright, poet and actor and is regarded as one of the greatest writers of the English language. He was a frequent visitor to Dover when he was writing his play, King Lear. One of the white cliffs have been named Shakespeare Cliff after him. The dramatist's 'King's Men' performed his plays in Dover in 1609. It is possible that Shakespeare was among the actors.

Aphra Behn (1874 - 1948)

Behn is believed to have been born in the Canterbury area. She was the first English woman to earn a living writing and was also a spy for Charles II.

Thomas Sidney Cooper (1803 - 1902)

Thomas Sidney Cooper was a painter renowned for his landscapes and paintings of farm animals. He was born in Saint Peter's Street, Canterbury and spent time in London and Brussels. He established an art school in Canterbury. He is buried in Saint Martin's churchyard in Canterbury.

William Burgess (1805 - 1861)

Burgess was an artist who lived at 14 Stembrook, Dover. He sketched and painted Dover landscapes as well as teaching art.

Charles Dickens (1812 - 1870)

Dickens is regarded as the greatest writer of the Victorian era. He has strong links with Kent and in the summer of 1852, rented a house for several months (10 Camden Crescent). He described the place as: "the sea is very fine, and the walks are quite remarkable" in Volume 1 of his Letters of Charles Dickens.

William Burges (1827 - 1881)

Burges was an architect and designer who worked within the gothic revival style. As well as architecture he also designed metalwork, sculpture, jewellery, furniture and stained glass. He went on over 50 pilgrimages to Italy and France for creative inspiration. William worked on the Maison Dieu along with Ambrose Poynter. Emulating the original medieval style of the grotesque animals, they were instrumental in the development of the building including the Connaught Hall, mayoral and official offices.

Joseph Conrad (1857 - 1924)

Conrad is regarded as one of England's greatest novelists. He was born in, what was at the time, Poland but is now in Ukraine. He lived in a number of locations in Kent and died in Bishopsbourne.

Mary Tourtel (1874 - 1948)

Mary Tourtel wrote children's books including the Rupert the Bear series. She was born at 52 Palace Street, Canterbury and spent her final years at 63 Ivy Lane. The Rupert series were originally cartoon strips in The Express newspaper and illustrated by her husband Herbert. She is buried in Saint Martin's churchyard and there is a display about her work in The Beaney Museum.

Henry Moore (1898 - 1986)

Moore is an internationally renowned artists specialising in bronze and stone sculptures and was inspired by the church at Barfrestone and flints on the Downs. He had a holiday cottage in Barfrestone and later lived in Kingston.

Jocelyn Brooke (1908 - 1966)

Brooke was born in Sandgate near Folkestone and later lived in Bishopsbourne. He wrote about and explored the area in search of orchids.

Ian Fleming (1908 - 1964)

Fleming was an author who spent some time living in Kent which features in a number of his books. His experience working for the Intellingence Service was put to good use in his best-selling novels about the spy, James Bond. He also wrote one children's book, Chitty Chitty Bang Bang in which the car flies over Canterbury.

Sun dial on Saint Mary's church, Dover

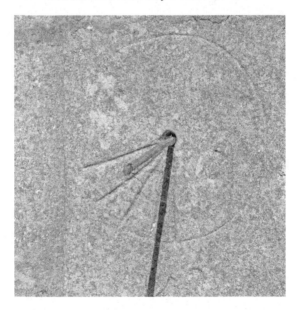

Mass dial at Barfrestone church

Historical Timeline

13,000 BC Paleolithic or Old Stone Age

9,500 BC   The Mesolithic or Middle Stone Age

6,000 BC   Water levels rise separating the British Isles from mainland Europe

4,000 BC   Neolithic or New Stone Age

2,300 BC   The Bronze Age – people arriving from Europe bring with them the skills to make tools from bronze and copper

2,200 BC   People are now being buried in round Barrows

750 BC   The Iron Age

600 BC   The Celts arrive and settle in the British Isles

54 AD   Julius Caesar and his Roman army briefly invade the British Isles

43 AD   Full Roman Invasion

410 AD   The Roman army leaves Britain to be ruled by the Romano-British

449 AD   Anglo-Saxon England begins with Hengist and Horsa landing and settling in Kent.

550 AD   Birth of King Ethelbert

565 AD   Birth of Queen Bertha (later Saint Bertha)

597 AD   Augustine lands in Kent at the invitation of King Ethelbert and Bertha, his wife. He begins converting the Anglo-Saxons to Christianity

598 AD   The first English monastery is built in Canterbury

601 AD   Death of Queen Bertha

615 AD   Death of King Ethelbert

865 AD   A Viking army lands in England and attempts to conquer the country

1016 AD   Cnut, a Danish prince, invades England and becomes the new king

1042 AD   Edward the Confessor becomes king and regains rule for the Anglo-Saxons

1066 AD   Edward the Confessor dies and Harold Godwinson becomes King, Harald Hardrada King of Norway arrives to claim the throne but is defeated by King Harold near York

Duke William of Normandy defeats King Harold at the Battle of Hastings and begins the Norman Conquest

1069 AD	Work commences on the Bayeux Tapestry
1086 AD	King William has the country surveyed to established who owns what in England known as the Domesday Book.
1087 AD	King William dies and William II becomes King.
1096 AD	The start of the Crusades
1162 AD	Thomas Becket becomes Archbishop of Canterbury
1170 AD	Thomas Becket is murdered
1173 AD	Thomas Becket is canonised
1215 AD	The signing of the Magna Carta at Runnymede
1272 AD	The end of the Crusades
1348 AD	The Black Death
1485 AD	The Reign of the Tudors
1536 AD	The Dissolution of the Monasteries begins.
1603 AD	The reign of the Stuarts
1605 AD	The Gunpowder Plot to blow up House of Lords is foiled
1642 AD	Beginning of English Civil War
1649 AD	England has no king or queen after the Execution of Charles 1. Oliver Cromwell takes over
1660 AD	Charles II takes over and becomes King
1714 AD	The Reign of the Georgians
1756 AD	Beginning of The Seven Years War between Britain and France
1760 AD	onwards - Beginning of the Industrial Revolution
1837 AD	Beginning of the Victorian era
1901 AD	Beginning of the Edwardian era
1914-18	The First World War
1939-45	The Second World War

Walk 1 – Dover to Kearsney (Seafront to Maison Dieu Road)

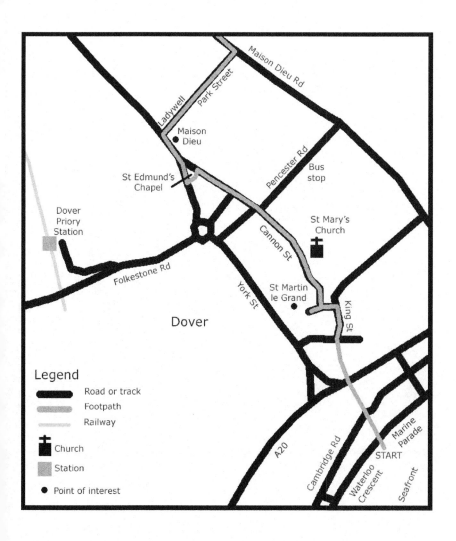

Walk 1 – Dover to Kearsney (Maison Dieu Road to London Road)

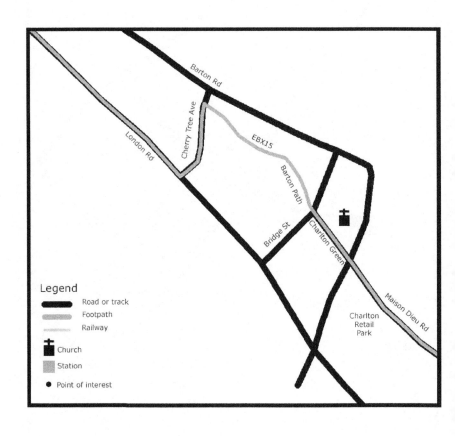

Walk 1 – Dover to Kearsney (London Road to Crabble Corn Mill)

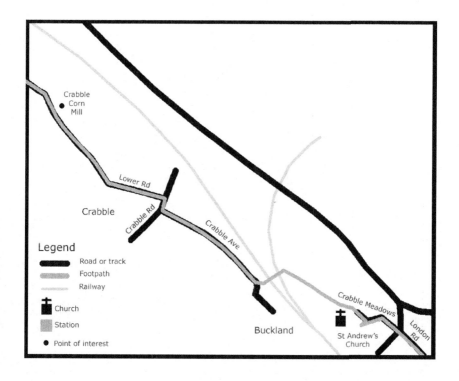

Walk 1 – Dover to Kearsney (Crabble Corn Mill to Kearsney)

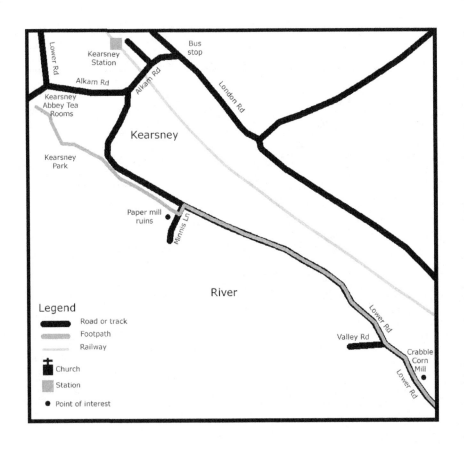

Walk 1 – Dover to Kearsney

3.21 miles

The pilgrimage starts at the North Downs Way marker on the seafront. It is close to here that many pilgrims from the Continent would have landed.

The Seafront

Start at the North Downs Way marker / Cross Channel Swimming sculpture called On the Crest of a Wave, Waterloo Crescent, Dover CT16 1LA

Over the centuries, the seafront at Dover has changed.

Look out for:
- ☐ Hag stones on the beach
- ☐ Shells on the beach
- ☐ Ferries departing and arriving at the port
- ☐ The White Cliffs

The A20 Underpass

Seafront to A20 Underpass and River Dour – 0.09 miles

The route passes over the River Dour as it flows into Wellington Dock and under the A20. It has changed course over the years. It is at this point that a Bronze Age boat was discovered. The boat is now in the Dover Museum.

Look out for:
- ☐ River Dour
- ☐ Blue plaque marking the discovery site of the Bronze Age Boat
- ☐

Dover Museum

A20 Underpass to Dover Museum and St Martin Le Grand – 0.13 miles

Market Square, Dover CT16 1PH – www.dovermuseum.co.uk

The museum charts the history of Dover and houses the Bronze Age boat that was discovered in Dover.

Saint Martin le Grand ruins

York Street, Market Square, Dover CT16 1PH

The ruins of Saint Martin le Grand can be viewed from the raised area in front of the Discovery Centre. Originally built in Saxon times, Saint Martin le Grand and it's monastery were rebuilt by the Normans. The church and monastery dedicated to Saint Martin was said to rival Canterbury Cathedral. The reformation brought on the beginning of it's destruction. The bells, clock and seats were given to Saint Mary's church. The town's defences were bolstered using materials from the monastery.

Look out for:
- ☐
- ☐
- ☐
- ☐

Saint Mary the Virgin church

Dover Museum to St Mary's – 0.09 miles

Cannon Street Dover CT16 1BY – www.stmarysdover.org.uk

Dating from the Saxon era, Saint Mary the Virgin is almost 1,000 years old. Rebuilt by the Normans, the tower and three bays of the arcades are the oldest parts of the building. There is evidence of a Roman bath house beneath the foundations. The church has been extended three times and the tower is a mix of early and late Norman with a more modern spire.

There is a mural depicting the visit to Jesus by the three wise men above the Saxon stone arch by a Dutch artist painted in 1889.

Look out for:
☐ Sundial
☐ Zeebrugge window
☐ Mural
☐

Saint Edmund of Abingdon Chapel

St Mary's to St Edmund's – 0.19 miles

Priory Road, Dover CT16 1BB – www.stedmundschapel.co.uk

The chapel, one of the smallest in England, belonged to Saint Martin's Priory and was attached to the pauper's cemetery. It was consecrated in 1253 by Richard, Bishop of Chichester to Saint Edmund, Archbishop of Canterbury.

Richard of Chichester died at the Maison Dieu shortly after preaching and collecting money for the 7th crusade. His relics were placed in a cist under the alter and his shrine became the third most visited in England after Becket.

Early pilgrims would have passed the chapel on their way to the shrine of Saint Thomas Becket at Canterbury Cathedral.

After the dissolution of the monasteries in the 16th Century the chapel had a variety of uses until it's renovation and reconsecration in 1968.

The chapel was built at ground level but over the centuries the road has gained height.

Look out for:
- ☐ Crosses carved into window frames
- ☐ location of shrine of Richard of Chichester
- ☐
- ☐

Dover War Memorial

St Edmund's to the War Memorial and Maison Dieu House – 0.03 miles

3 Biggin Street, Dover CT16 1BD

The Dover War Memorial was designed by Richard Goulden who was a veteran of the Great War. Unveiled in 1924 it has a grappling iron used in the raid by the Dover Patrol to block the Port of Zeebrugge and prevent the German submarines leaving the port on 23 April 1918.

Look out for:
- ☐
- ☐
- ☐
- ☐

Maison Dieu House

Directly behind the war memorial is Maison Dieu House. Now the town council offices, Maison Dieu house was built in 1665 for use as the office of the Agent Victualler of the Navy.

Look out for:
- ☐
- ☐
- ☐
- ☐

Maison Dieu

War Memorial to Maison Dieu – 0.01 miles

Biggin Street, Dover CT16 1DL - www.maisondieudover.org.uk

Maison Dieu is dedicated to Saint Mary and was founded in 1203 by Hubert de Burgh to provide hospitality to pilgrims travelling to the shrine of Saint Thomas Becket in Canterbury.

The tower to the right of the main steps is part of the original Maison Dieu and the tops of the arches on the tower illustrate how the pavement has risen over the centuries.

It is a grade I listed building and has had many functions over the years including town hall, gaol, military store, museum and concert hall. In the Stone Hall the stained glass windows were installed in 1873 and illustrate historic events.

The Maison Dieu was restored and extended by Ambrose Poynter and William Burges. The additional building was an assembly hall called the Connaught Hall which also housed the civic offices.

Hanging outside the main entrance is the Zeebrugge Bell which was given to the town by the Belgian King in 1918 to mark the Zeebrugge Raid in WWI.

Under the Victorian extension lies a well dedicated to Saint Mary. The well remained in use until the 19th Century.

Look out for:
- □ Carved shield of Saint Martin of Tours on exterior
- □ Zebrugge bell
- □
- □

Charlton

Maison Dieu to Castleton Retail Park in the centre of Charlton (Morrisions supermarket) – 0.37 miles

This is the first village outside of the original Dover boundaries. The River Dour passes underneath what is now Castleton Shopping Centre – once The Green and centre of the village.

Evidence suggests that the Dour was navigable up to Charton in Roman times.

The Chalybeate spring rises in Chartlon and flows into a tributary of the Dour. This lead to the bottling of the water by Stephen Elms who also established a sweet factory here.

Look out for:
- □ River Dour
- □
- □
- □

Barton Path

Castleton Retail Park to Barton Path – 0.14 miles

The route follows Barton Path along the river. The five mile long River Dour rises at Watersend in Temple Ewell and flows through the villages and town of Dover to the English Channel at Wellington Dock. Fed by nine springs, including a tributary that rises in Drellingore in the Alkam valley, the river is a rare habitat for flora and fauna and one of only 200 chalk streams in the world. The exceptional water quality supports a colony of brown trout. The river supports plants such as crowfoot and starworts.

It has supported water-powered industries including flour, paper, oil seed and sawmills.

Look out for:
- ☐ Brown trout
- ☐ Yellow flag iris
- ☐ Moorhens
- ☐ Swans
- ☐ Ducks
- ☐

Buckland

Barton Path to Cherry Tree Avenue, Buckland – 0.24 miles

Buckland was once a village and is now a suburb of Dover.

Look out for:
- ☐ Converted Flour Mill on London Road
- ☐
- ☐
- ☐

Saint Andrew's Church, Buckland

Cherry Tree Avenue to St Andrew's – 0.48 miles

Crabble Meadows, Dover CT17 0TR
www.bucklandchurchesdover.org.uk

The Domesday Book records a church on the site in 1086, however, the current church dates from 1180. It is dedicated to Saint Andrew who is the patron saint of fishermen and singers.

The north chapel is dedicated to Catherine of Alexandria. She gives her name to the Catherine Wheel firework as she was tortured by being splayed on a wheel and then beheaded.

The south chapel is dedicated to a local monk, Saint Thomas de la Hale, who was martyred by French raiders at the Priory of Saint Martin, He was buried at Dover Priory church and soon after his death, miracles were recorded which attracted many pilgrims heading to the shrine of Saint Thomas Becket.

In the churchyard is an ancient tree is a common yew with a girth measuring 8.9 metres. TR3048542689. On yew trees the female and male flowers grow on separate trees between March and April. The seeds are in a red berry-like structure called an aril which is open at the tip. Yew trees contain highly poisonous taxane alkaloids which have been used in anti-cancer drugs. Most churches were built next to a yew tree.

Look out for:
☐ Buckland Yew
☐
☐
☐

Crabble Corn Mill

St Andrew's to Crabble Corn Mill – 0.63 miles

Crabble Corn Mill, Lower Road, Dover, CT17 0UY
01304 823 292 – www.ccmt.org.uk

Crabble corn mill is one of the finest examples of a working Georgian watermill in Europe. It was built in 1812 and occupies a site that has had mills for 800 years.

Look out for:
□ O/S benchmark
□
□
□

Kearsney

River to Kearsney Abbey Tea Rooms – 0.75 miles

The name Kearsney is derived from the French word cressionière meaning place where watercress grows. The river Dour is joined by one of it's tributaries from the Alkam valley in the Kearsney Abbey parkland where they form a lake.

Kearsney Abbey can be traced back to the Norman Conquest when it was known as Castney Court and was part of the Barony of Saye. The current park was created by John Minet Fector who built a grand mansion on the site between 1820 and 1822. The only remaining part of the building is the former billiard room which is now a café.

Bats including pipistrelle can be seen feeding at dusk.

The walk passes a large Cedar of Lebanon surrounded by a fence. It is believed to be around 160 years old and one of the oldest in the country. It is an ancient tree with a girth measuring 9.55 metres. Cedars have both male and female reproductive organs on the same plant.

Look out for:
□ Cedar of Lebanon
□ Swans
□
□

Kearsney Abbey Tea Rooms, Alkam Road, Temple Ewell, CT16 3EG – 01304 829 046 – www.kearsneyparks.co.uk

Public Transport – Bus (London Road) to Dover or Canterbury (0.27 miles) - Train – Kearsney station – to Dover or Canterbury (0.26 miles)

Walk 2 – Kearsney to Shepherdswell (Kearsney Abbey Tea Rooms to Nature Reserve)

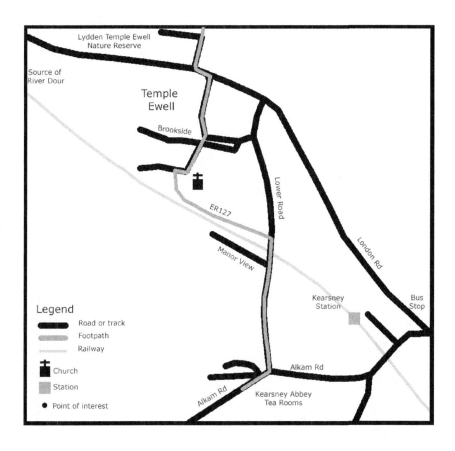

Lydden Temple Ewell
Nature Reserve

Source of
River Dour

Temple
Ewell

Brookside

ER127

Lower Road

Manor View

London Rd

Kearsney
Station

Bus
Stop

Alkam Rd

Alkam Rd

Kearsney Abbey
Tea Rooms

Legend

Road or track
Footpath
Railway
Church
Station
Point of interest

Walk 2 – Kearsney to Shepherdswell (full route)

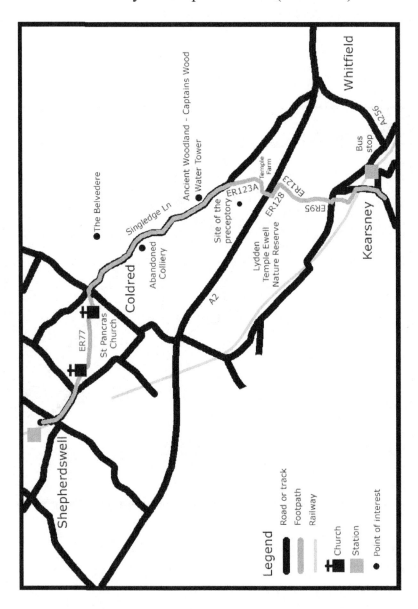

Walk 2 – Kearsney to Shepherdswell

4.27 miles

The second walk starts at Kearsney Abbey Tearooms and heads up the hill through Temple Ewell and onto the Downs.

Temple Ewell

Temple Ewell can be traced back to Roman times when Watling Street was being laid. Watling Street runs from Dover to Wales.

Temple Ewell was under Norman ownership after 1066 when it was known as Ewelle or Etwelle. At the time the village included five watermills. "Temple" was added to the village name in 1163 to mark the new ownership by the Knights Templar.

The Knights Templar also built a corn mill on the River Dour which was subsequently rebuilt in 1535. At the time the village was mainly a farming community.

The village has now spread along the River Dour towards the next village of Kearsney.

Saint Peter and Saint Paul Church

Abbey Tea Rooms to St Peter and St Paul's – 0.37 miles

1 Church Hill, Temple Ewell CT16 3GL

Originally Norman in style and built by The Knights Templar the building has evolved with major restauration in the 19th Century. The cross emblem of the Knights Templar can be seen in the porch of the church. There are fragments of Swiss and German (16th and 17th Century) enamel glass in the chancel which is more usually seen in churches in France and Germany.

Look out for:

☐ O/S Benchmark
☐ Templar Cross
☐ Headstones with scull and crossbones
☐ Norman doorway

Lydden Temple Ewell Nature Reserve

St Peter and St Paul's to Nature Reserve – 0.35 miles

London Road, Temple Ewell CT16 3DE
www.kentwildlifetrust.org.uk

The nature reserve is managed by the Kent Wildlife Trust. It is a steep slope with diverse grasslands in summer populated by: orchids, over 20 species of butterflies, crickets and grasshoppers including the Wart Biter Cricket.

Look out for:

☐ Orchids
☐ Butterflies
☐
☐

Temple Farm

Temple Ewell Nature Reserve to Temple Farm – 0.68 miles

The farm takes it's name from the nearby site of the preceptory for the Knights Templar and consists of 18th and 19th Century farmhouse.

Across a field in some woodland is the site of the Knights Templar Preceptory (c1185). Between 1964 - 1966 excavations revealed remains of medieval buildings on the site. According to Hasted, they were destroyed in the early 18th Century. The building contained 7 rooms and a small chapel. Nearby is a Romano-British pit which produced pottery.

Guilford Colliery remains

Temple Farm to Guilford Colliery remains – 1.12 miles

All that remains of the colliery is a brick engine house. In the early 20th Century three shafts were sunk but the site was abandoned in 1921 without mining for coal due to water ingress.

The engine house has been renovated and is now a wedding venue called The Winding House (Singledge Lane, Coldred CT15 5AG).

Saint Pancras Church, Coldred

Guilford Colliery Remains to St Pancras – 0.55 miles

Church Road, Coldred, CT15 5AG
www.bewsboroughparish.org

The church is a Grade I listed building believed to be Saxon or early Norman. Standing within earthworks believed to be a motte and bailey.

Next to the church is Coldred Manor which appears to be on the possible mutilated motte and bailey castle linked to the church. The manor was owned by Odo, Bishop of Bayeux at the time of the Domesday Book. Excavation has produced Roman and Saxon remains.

Saint Pancras was a Christian brought up in Rome at the end of the 3rd Century and, after the death of his parents, was brought up by an uncle. During the Diocletian's persecution he was beheaded at the age of 14. He is venerated in England because Saint Augustine dedicated his first church to him. The ruins of the church lie within the grounds of Saint Augustine's Abbey in Canterbury.

The route joins the North Downs Way / Via Francigena behind the church where the motte and bailey can be seen more clearly. A motte and bailey is an early medieval fortification.

Look out for:
☐ O/S Benchmark
☐ Ditch of the motte and bailey
☐
☐

Shepherdswell

St Pancras, Coldred to St Andrew's, Shepherdswell – 0.90 miles

The village name has changed over the centuries and is now known as either Shepherdswell or Sibertswold which means 'wood of Sibert'. The church and Bell Inn sit around the village green.

Saint Andrew's Church

St Andrew's Church, The Green, Shepherdswell CT15 7LQ
www.bewsboroughparish.org

The current church is Victorian and dates from 1863. However, there are references of a church on the site in 944. The first church is believed to have been a wooden Saxon building which was later replaced by a two celled Romanesque church in the 12th Century. The stained glass in the east windows depict the ascension of Christ and the four evangelists.

Look out for:
☐ O/S Benchmark
☐
☐
☐

The Bell Inn, 22 Church Hill, Shepherdswell CT15 7LG – 01304 830 661

The East Kent Railway

St Andrew's to Shepherdswell Station – 0.38 miles

East Kent Railway, Station Road, Shepherdswell CT15 7PD
Café and tourist railway – 01304 832 042
www.eastkentrailway.co.uk

The East Kent Railway was originally built (between 1911 and 1917) to serve the local Kent coal mines and currently runs a tourist service between Shepherdswell and Eythorne. Entry to the station is free and there is a café. The site is bordered by the Knees Woodland with it's nature walks and picnic area.

Walk 3 – Shepherdswell to Womenswold

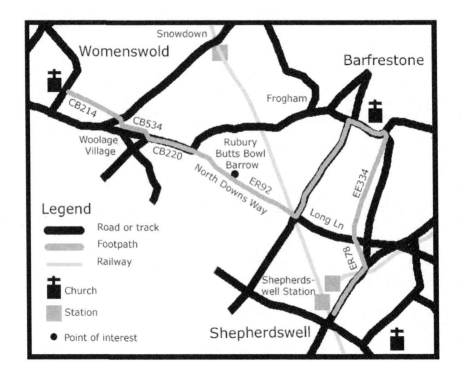

Walk 3 – Shepherdswell to Womanswold

4.45 miles

The walk departs Shepherdswell station and picks up a footpath heading out of the village across undulating farmland.

Barfrestone

Shepherdswell station to Barfrestone church – 1.54 miles

The hamlet of Barfrestone has been inhabited for over 1,000 years. The name means 'hamlet on ash tree hill' which highlights it's position on some of the highest ground in the area. At the time of the Domesday Book it was owned by Odo, Bishop of Bayeux.

Henry Moore, sculptor, had a holiday cottage (Jasmine Cottage) in the village and was inspired by the church. He later moved down the road to Kingston.

Saint Nicholas Church

Eythorne Road, Barfrestone CT15 7JQ
www.bewsboroughparish.org

The first church to be built on the site was in around 1080, after the Norman Conquest. The only evidence of this is in the West wall. In around 1175-80 the church was rebuilt in it's current form of ornate stone. The elaborately carved Caen stone is decorated with figures, animals, nature and mythical creatures. The church received a much needed and sympathetic restauration in 1840-41. In 1958 John Betjeman wrote that Barfrestone church was "the best Norman church in Kent."

In the churchyard is an ancient tree, a common yew with a girth of 5.23 metres. TR2641650154

Look out for:
- ☐ Mass dial
- ☐ Wheel window
- ☐ Church bell in a tree
- ☐

The Wrong Turn, micro pub, Envirograf House, 2 Pie Factory Road, Birchfield, Barfrestone CT15 7JG – 07522 554 118 – phone to check opening times. Pie Factory Road is on the right after the church.

Rubury Butts

Barfrestone church to Rubury Butts – 1.54 miles

Three bowl barrows alongside the North Downs Way in a small wood. Believed to be from the Bronze Age. At this point the North Downs Way is known as Long Lane and is thought to be either Roman or earlier in origin.

The barrows are in a row and are burial mounds.

Look out for:
- ☐ Bowl barrows
- ☐
- ☐

Woolage Village

Rubury Butts to Woolage Village – 0.71 miles

The village is relatively new having been built to house miners from the nearby mine at Snowdown.

In the children's play area next to the footpath for the Via Francigena is an artwork called 'After the Black Gold' which was created for the Via Francigena Art Trail which runs between Dover and Canterbury. The artists, Ryan Cook and Sam Little, were inspired by the lean-to roof pitches at Snowdown Colliery.

Look out for:
☐ 'After the Black Gold' artwork
☐
☐

To Snowdown for trains to Canterbury and Dover – 0.94 miles

Womenswold

Woolage Village to Womenswold Church – 0.77 miles

Womenswold is of Anglo-Saxon origin, appearing in a charter of 824 as Wimlincga Wold. To the South West of Womenswold is Denne Hill which was once owned by the Knights Templar.

The composer and diarist, John Ward (1752-1828), spent some time in the village living at the family home of Nethersole House (or farmhouse). He is the author of The John Marsh Journals.

Look out for:
☐ Thatched cottage
☐

Saint Margaret of Antioch Church, Womanswold

The Street, Womenswold CT4 6HE
www.barhamdownschurches.org.uk

The church is built in the early English style and 12th Century in origin and is unusual in design as it has no side aisles. In the sanctuary there are three medieval sedila set into the south wall. These are seat for the ministers.

The church is dedicated to Saint Margaret who was popular with knights returning from the crusades. There is a small head stone believed to be Saint Margaret on the exterior of the church above the central lancet.

Saint Margaret is the patron saint of childbirth. According to legend, she was the daughter of a pagan priest in Antioch in what is now modern-day Turkey. She converted to Christianity whereupon her father threw her out of his house. She then became a shepherdess. The local prefect was infatuated with her beauty but she spurned him and he threw her into prison. While in prison she met the devil in the form of a dragon. The dragon swallowed her but the cross she held in her hand irritated his throat so much so that he disgorged her. Unsuccessful attempts were then made to execute and drown her and while these attempts were being undertaken, she converted thousands of spectators to Christianity. She was then beheaded.

Look out for:
- ☐ O/S Benchmark
- ☐ Three sedillas
- ☐
- ☐

To Snowdown for trains (1.33 miles)
To Adisham Rd (cemetery) for the 89 bus (0.55 miles)

Cross carved into doorway of Barfrestone Church

Barfrestone church

Walk 4 – Womenswold to Kingston

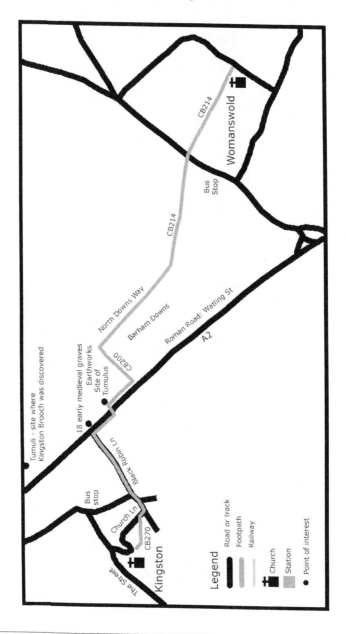

Legend

Road or track
Footpath
Railway

Church
Station
Point of interest

Walk 4 – Womenswold to Kingston

2.96 miles

Bus stop – 89 Stagecoach to Canterbury – at the Cemetery on Adisham Road after Womenswold church. The station at Snowdown for trains to Dover and Canterbury.

From Womenswold the walk takes the North Downs Way out along Barham Downs where it enters the Kent Downs AONB.

Barham Downs

Womenswold to Barham Downs – 0.89 miles

There are earthworks believed to be early Iron age (800BC - 401BC) on the crest of Barhams Downs ridge. There is a slight platform which lies over the ancient trackway that ran along the ridge. Pre-Roman potsherd (broken ceramic material) has been found on the site – some of which is held at Maidstone Museum.

Before the horse bridge over the A2 there is a Bronze Age (2350BC - 701BC) round barrow. The tumulus has been destroyed but there is still some evidence of it.

Further on along Barham Downs is a more significant tumuli where the Kingston Brooch was discovered. The Kingston Brooch was a piece of Anglo-Saxon jewellery (7th Century) which was discovered in a tumulus on Kingston Downs. The brooch is made of gold with blue glass, white shell and garnets. This is now housed in the World Museum of Liverpool.

Look out for:
□ Wildflowers
□ Insects

☐
☐

Watling Street (A2)

Barham Downs to Horse Bridge over A2 – 1.52 miles

Watling Street was originally a Celtic road but was subsequently taken over and improved by the Romans. The road runs from Dover, through Canterbury and London and onto Wales. For most of the stretch between Dover and Canterbury the road has been absorbed by the A2.

Kingston

Horse Bridge over A2 to Kingston Church – 0.73 miles

Kingston lies in the narrow Bourne valley and sits on the southern side of Barham Downs.

In Saxon times the settlement of Kingston belonged to the King. This was when Kent was an independent kingdom. The village was not mentioned in the Domesday Book as it appears to have been included with the other nearby villages.

Henry Moore lived at Burcroft, Marley Lane on the outskirts of the village from 1935 - 1940. The house had extensive grounds so he could sculpt outside. The house has subsequently been renamed the Orchard. Between 1938 - 1939 Henry Moore and his assistant, Bernard Meadows, produced 18 - 20 small figures (Reclining Figures) at the house.

The Black Robin Pub, Covet Lane, Kingston CT4 6HS – 01227 830 230 – www.theblackrobin.com

The Black Robin has been a pub since 1741 and was named after a local highwayman who was hung on the gallows on Barham Downs/Barham crossroads. 'Black Robin' was a Kentish slang term for a smuggler and between 1820 - 1826 there were many smuggling gangs working in the Elham valley.

Look out for:
☐ The Nailbourne (an intermittently flowing river)
☐
☐
☐

Bus stop Stagecoach 89 and 17 direction Canterbury.

Saint Giles Church

Church Lane, Kingston, CT4 6HY
www.barhamdownschurches.org.uk

The early medieval church was remodelled at the beginning of the 20th Century. It is built of flint and the wall of the nave and chancel have been dated to Saxon-Norman times. To the right of the north door (entrance) is a well-preserved holy water stoup.

The font dates from the 13th Century. At some stage in the 18th Century, it was discarded and used as a feeding trough by a local farmer. It eventually made it's way back in to the church in 1931 when it was reconsecrated.

The church is named after Saint Giles who was an 8th Century hermit living in a forest near the river Rhone. Traditionally his is the patron saint of disabled people.

In 1771, the Reverend Bryan Faussett discovered the Kingston Brooch on the Downs above Kingston.

Look out for:
☐
☐
☐
☐

Decorative grave in Kingston churchyard

Coldred church

Walk 5 – Kingston to Patrixbourne

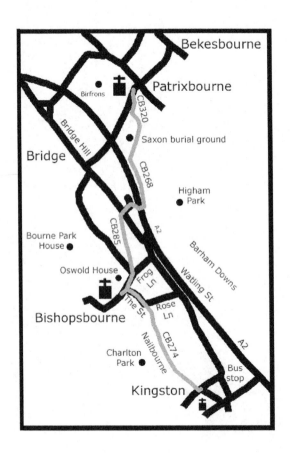

Walk 5 – Kingston to Patrixbourne

2.96 miles

Leaving Kingston, pick up the footpath of the Elham Valley Way and Old Way pilgrimage route from Southampton to Canterbury. The route follows the Nailbourne along the valley floor.

The Nailbourne

The Nailbourne is a river that runs every few years near Folkestone to beyond Wickhambreaux where it joins the Little Stour River.

At the time of the Domesday Book, the Nailbourne was a fully flowing river. At some stage during the 18th Century, it became a winterbourne (the term for an intermittently flowing river). It rises in a holy spring called Saint Eadburg's well in a field in the village of Lyminge. A possible reason for the change in water flow is that it's source is a spring above Folkestone which is the most active earthquake zone in the UK. It is possible that one or more earthquakes disrupted the waterflow.

Look out for:
□ Birds of prey
□

Charlton Park

Kingston Church to Charlton Parkland – 0.42 miles

The footpath passes through the grounds of Charlton Park which is a Grade II listed country house set in parkland. The main part of the house is Tudor and possibly incorporates earlier foundations. There are several wells adjacent to the house, one of which dates from the 15th Century.

The park hosted the Medicine Ball Caravan festival in August of 1970 in which Pink Floyd performed. The event was overshadowed by the Isle of Wight Festival. The Medicine Ball Caravan Tour was funded by Warner Brothers and this film was released in 1971 with little or no footage of the event at Charlton Park.

Look out for:
☐
☐

Bishopsbourne

Charlton Park to St Mary's – 0.74 miles

The village of Bishopsbourne lies further along the Nailbourne. It is first mentioned as the village of Burnam in 708AD. By 800AD Bishopsbourne was a thriving agricultural community with some of it coming under the ownership of Saint Augustine's and then the ownership of the Archbishop of Canterbury. In the Domesday Book (1086) Bishopsbourne had two watermills and 117 dwellings. At that time the Nailbourne was a fully flowing river.

The Mermaid Inn, The Street, Bishopsbourne CT4 5HX
01227 830 581 – www.mermaidinnbishopsbourne.com
Once a tap house for the local estate workers.

Richard Hooker (1554 - 1600) was the rector and author and was a theologian whose work underpinned the Elizabethan Anglican movement.

Jocelyn Brooke lived in the village at Ivy Cottage in The Street. He wrote about and explored the area in search of orchids.

Joseph Conrad lived at Oswolds, a large country house next to the church in the village. For a year in the 1930's the author Alec Waugh (1898 - 1981) lived in Joseph Conrad's house. Alec is the less well-known brother of Evelyn Waugh.

Reverend Joseph Bankcroft Reade (1801 - 1870) was the rector between 1863 - 1870 and is buried in the churchyard close to the north wall of the church. He was an amateur scientist and pioneer in photography. He developed the use of lenses to focus on a specimen under a microscope. He used a chemical process to increase the light sensitivity of photographic paper and he was the first Englishman to photograph the moon.

Look out for:
☐ Village hall named after Joseph Conrad
☐ Ivy Cottage in The Street
☐

Saint Mary's Church

Crowscamp Road, Bishopsbourne CT4 5JB
www.barhamdownschurches.org.uk

The first church is mentioned in the Domesday Book however there is no other record of it. The current church was built in the 13th Century and was restored in the 19th Century.

Above the nave are remains of early 14th Century wall paintings. Around the altar are mosaic tiles in the style of William Morris and William de Morgan. Carved on the pillars are medieval graffiti as well as some crosses and daisy wheels.

Look out for:
- ☐ O/S Benchmark
- ☐ Medieval graffiti
- ☐ Medieval wall paintings

Tadpole Tearooms, Frog Lane, Bishopsbourne, CT4 5HR
01227 830 178

Bourne Park

Bishopsbourne Church to Bourne Park – 0.19 miles

The route takes the footpath back onto the Downs with a view across the valley to Bourne Park. This Queen Anne country house is situated in the valley and surrounded by parkland. It was built in the early 18th Century of red brick and stone. Remains of a large Roman villa have been discovered under the old cricket pitch in Bourne Park.

Look out for:
- ☐
- ☐
- ☐

Higham Park

Bourne Park to Higham Park – 0.74 miles

The current house was built in around 1768 and incorporates elements from earlier years. The Higham Estate originally stretched as far as Upper Hardres and Wingham. The Grade II building was built in the neoclassical style with a Palladian front piece.

Thomas Culpepper (c1514 - 1541) was a famous author and herbalist in the reign of Henry VIII who owned the house from 1534.

Wolfgang Amadeus Mozart (1719 - 1787), composer, visited the house in 1765, when he was 9 years old, and performed on the piano in the music room.

Count Louis Zborowski (1895 - 1924) inherited the estate which then became known for the creation of racing cars including the first aero-engine racing cars including Chitty Bang Bang in 1921.

Ian Fleming was a regular visitor and named his only children's book after the car: Chitty Chitty Bang Bang. Ian Fleming was a later visitor to the estate and was inspired by the cars.

Look out for:
- ☐
- ☐
- ☐

Bifrons

Bifrons was a country house set in parkland between Bridge and Patrixbourne. It was built in the early 1660s and remodelled in 1770. The house became the home of the last mistress of George IV, Elizabeth Conyngham, Marchioness Conyngham, in 1820.

In 1866 and 1867 excavations were made in an Anglo-Saxon Cemetery at Bifrons. These can now be found in the Maidstone Museum.

Patrixbourne

Higham Park to St Mary's – 1.04 miles

The village has links with Normandy. The manor and village were owned by the Patric family and gave their name to the village. They came from near Flers in Normandy and William Patric was a knight and landowner.

Ian Fleming lived for a short while within the parish at The Old Palace, Bekesbourne (1960-62) which lies along the Nailbourne just beyond the village.

Look out for:
□
□
□

Saint Mary's Church

Patrixbourne Road, Patrixbourne CT4 5BP
www.bridgechurchgroup.co.uk

There is a brief mention of the church in the Domesday Book. In the 12th Century it was a two-celled building like many in East Kent and Normandy.

Further highlighting the links with France, the church was given to a priory near Rouen in around 1200. The south door has a decorative triangular gable which is similar to churches in Normandy with links to the Patric family.

It has the addition of the Bifrons chapel and, unusually, a tower midway along the south aisle. In the Bifrons chapel is a window with 18 panels of Swiss enamel glass similar to those in the chancel of Saint Peter and Saint Paul church at Temple Ewell.

The position of the elaborate Romanesque south door is also unusual. The wheel window is similar to the one at Barfrestone, each with decorated spokes.

Look out for:

- [ ] O/S Benchmark
- [ ] Wheel Window
- [ ] Bees
- [ ] Mass dial

Train from Bekesbourne station to Canterbury or Dover (0.76 miles)

Bishopsbourne

Wheel window on Saint Mary's church, Patrixbourne

Walk 6 – Patrixbourne to the outskirts of Canterbury

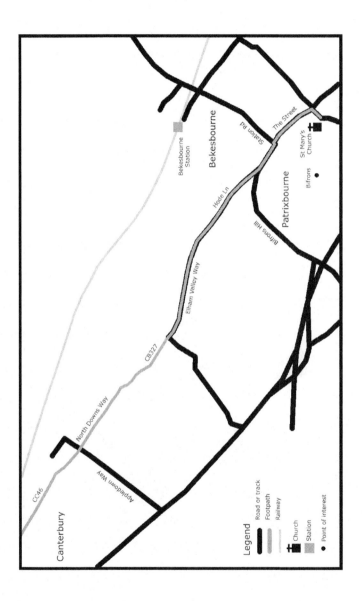

Walk 6 – Outskirts of Canterbury to Canterbury Cathedral

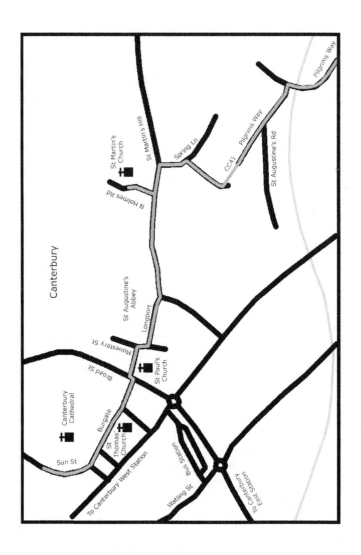

Walk 6 – Patrixbourne to Canterbury

3.48 miles

Leaving Patrixbourne the route continues along the North Downs way and out of the Kent Downs AONB.

Bekesbourne station to Patrixbourne church 0.76 miles

Look out for:
- ☐ Lion cottage, The Street
- ☐ Elephant cottage, The Street
- ☐
- ☐

Saint Martin's Church

Patrixbourne Church to St Martins – 2.78 miles

1 N Holmes Road, Canterbury CT1 1QJ – www.martinpaul.org

Saint Martin's Church is the oldest parish church in England and has been a place of continual Christian worship for 1400 years. Along with Canterbury Cathedral and Saint Augustine's it is part of the Canterbury UNESCO World Heritage Site. Before the arrival of Saint Augustine, it was Queen Bertha's chapel.

The Grade I listed building was originally Roman (late 6th Century) and has been extended over the years. The nave was built in the 7th Century with further extensions in the 12th, 13th and 14th Centuries.

In the churchyard is a notable tree called a blue atlas astor with a girth measuring 5.3 metres. Also in the churchyard are the graves of author, Mary Tourtel, and artist, Thomas Sydney Cooper.

Look out for:
- ☐ O/S Benchmark
- ☐ Gravestone of Mary Tourtel, author
- ☐ Gravestone of Thomas Sydney Cooper, artist
- ☐ 14th Century Christmatory

Saint Augustine's Abbey

St Martin's to St Augustine's – 0.27 miles

Longport, Canterbury CT1 1PF – www.english-heritage.org.uk

Founded in 598 by Saint Augustine, it was built in the Romanesque style. It was one of the most important monasteries in medieval England and developed into a thriving centre for learning before the dissolution of the monasteries. It may also have been where the Bayeux Tapestry was created.

Within the Abbey grounds lies the ruins of Saint Pancras church which was the first church to be consecrated by Saint Augustine. It had previously been a Roman temple in which Ethelbert had worshiped. The Abbey Gate is still standing.

Look out for:
- ☐
- ☐
- ☐
- ☐

Saint Paul's Without Church

9 Church Street, Canterbury CT1 1NH – www.martinpaul.org

Set outside the city walls, the single aisled church was developed around 1200.

The church was extended in the 13th and 14th Centuries but fell into disrepair after the reformation. In the 19th Century the church was remodelled by the gothic revivalist architect Sir Gilbert Scott.

Look out for:

☐

☐

☐

Saint Thomas' Church

St Augustine's to St Thomas' – 0.22 miles

59 Burgate, Canterbury CT1 2HJ
www.stthomasofcanterbury.com

Saint Thomas' church was built in 1875 and extended in 1963. The church has a shrine to Saint Thomas Becket and the relics of Saint Oscar Romero (1917 - 1980). In the Saints Chapel is a mural of the Canterbury saints.

Look out for:
☐ Mural of the Canterbury saints
☐ Relic of Saint Thomas Becket
☐

Canterbury Cathedral

St Thomas' to Canterbury Cathedral – 0.09 miles

The Precincts, Canterbury CT1 2EH
www.canterbury-cathedral.org

The cathedral was founded by Saint Augustine in 597 and is the cradle of the English church. A fire in 1067 destroyed most of the Anglo-Saxon cathedral. The Normans rebuilt the cathedral in 1077 with the crypt and the area of the North West Transept called the Martyrdom remaining.

After the death of Archbishop Thomas Becket, his shrine attracted pilgrims from all over Europe.

In 1215 Archbishop Stephen Langton (c1150 - 1228) was an important figure in the creation of the Magna Carta and thanks to his involvement Canterbury was one of five designated 'Magna Carta Towns'.

The miracle windows in Trinity Chapel illustrate the miracles of Saint Thomas Becket.

The cathedral has undergone damage over the years from the Civil War of the 1640s to World War II.

Look out for:
□ Bee boles
□ Site of the martyrdom of Saint Thomas Becket
□ Norman crypt
□ Miracle windows
□
□

Further Information

Bus Timetables - www.stagecoachbus.com/timetables

Train Timetables - www.southeasternrailway.co.uk

Accommodation

Airbnb.com – lists accommodation in the area including shepherd's huts in Barfrestone and Shepherdswell.

Royal Oak, Temple Ewell – CT17 0QU

Booking.com – The Stable at Womenswold CT4 6HD and The Annexe at Kingston CT4 6JA

Bed and Breakfast – Court Lodge Farmhouse B&B and Holiday Cottage, Bishopsbourne CT4 5JA www.courtlodgefarmhouse.co.uk – 01227 832 242

Beechborough B&B, Park Lane, Bishopsbourne CT4 5HY – www.beechborough.com – 01227 832 283

Tourism

Visit Kent - www.visitkent.co.uk

Destination Dover - www.destinationdover.org

White Cliffs – www.whitecliffscountryside.org.uk/

Visit Canterbury - www.canterbury.co.uk/VisitCanterbury

Kent Wildlife Trust – www.kentwildlifetrust.org

Additional Pilgrimage Attractions

Dover Castle - www.english-heritage.org.uk

Franciscan Gardens - www.franciscangardens.org.uk

Eastbridge Hospital - www.eastbridgehospital.org.uk

Kent Mining Museum – www.kentminingmuseum.co.uk

Useful Apps

Stagecoach buses app - www.stagecoachbus.com

Ordnance Survey app for maps - www.ordnancesurvey.co.uk

Ordnance Survey O/S locate for grid reference of exact location

What3Words app for exact location – www.what3words.com

Further Reading

Saint, Bishop and Concubine – How Canterbury made the Bayeux Tapestry by David Reekie

The Canterbury Rings by David Reekie

The Kent Downs by Dan Tuscon

Orchid Trilogy by Jocelyn Brooke

Chitty Chitty Bang Bang by Ian Fleming

Ruins of Saint Martin le Grand and The Discovery Centre

Bee bole at Canterbury Cathedral

About the Route Creators

Liz Garnett

Liz has been a travel photographer for over 29 years and is also a writer and North Downs Way Ambassador. She is based near Ashford in Kent. Liz was first drawn to pilgrimages in 2018 when she undertook the Tro Breiz pilgrimage which takes in the sites of the seven founding saints of Brittany in France.

In 2019 she persuaded Alexandra le Rossignol to join her in following the Augustine Camino through Kent. They brought together a group of artists to follow the route and respond to it with a series of exhibitions. They split the route into 14 short walks to allow the group to have time to observe and respond to their journey.

In 2022 Liz and Alexandra developed The Way of Saint Martin as a slow pilgrimage that is accessible by public transport and highlights the pilgrimage routes of medieval times between Dover and Canterbury.

Liz's travel photography is focussed on landscape and architecture in both the UK and France. Her art photography encompasses all formats as well as experimenting with different processes.

www.lizgarnett.com

Alexandra Le Rossignol

Alexandra is an artist living above the White Cliffs at Saint Margarets at Cliffe near Dover. For many years she has successfully made stained glass windows for churches in the Canterbury Diocese and beyond. However, she has now moved into a new direction having recently finished a three year course on iconography led by iconographer Peter Murphy.

Alexandra has always considered life as a pilgrimage and is inspired spiritually by edgelands – areas in the landscape where the boundary between heaven and earth seems very thin. Sacred spaces can be surprising places and the people we meet on the way. For Alex, her greatest joy has been the shared journey and fellowship with other pilgrims. Her biggest challenge has been believing that she can physically do the walk.

After successfully completing the Augustine Camino, Alexandra has shared her art journals and poetry and become involved with the wider ideas of pilgrimage. Planning a new route from Dover to Canterbury with Liz, she is exploring different ways of travel and hopes to produce a series of work inspired by medieval pilgrimage and bees. Although continuing icon work linked with the pilgrimage festival in September 2022, she is looking forward to expanding her work using mixed media.

Pilgrim Stamps from Churches

Notes

This book was printed on demand to help save the environment.

Printed in Great Britain
by Amazon

41978192R00050